ANCHOR BOOKS

A HIDDEN PROMISE

Edited by

Sarah Andrew

First published in Great Britain in 2001 by
ANCHOR BOOKS
Remus House,
Coltsfoot Drive,
Peterborough, PE2 9JX
Telephone (01733) 898102

All Rights Reserved

Copyright Contributors 2001

HB ISBN 1 85930 980 1
SB ISBN 1 85930 985 2

FOREWORD

Anchor Books is a small press, established in 1992, with the aim of promoting readable poetry to as wide an audience as possible.

We hope to establish an outlet for writers of poetry who may have struggled to see their work in print.

The poems presented here have been selected from many entries. Editing proved to be a difficult task and as the Editor, the final selection was mine.

I trust this selection will delight and please the authors and all those who enjoy reading poetry.

Sarah Andrew
Editor

CONTENTS

D IS FOR DEAD ON DEANSGATE

Danny the Deadleg
Disappeared for days
Then on a dark and damp
December evening on Deansgate
Danny the Deadleg was seen
Drunk and disorderly
Dressed in a dirty duffel
Later depressed and drifting
In a drugged daze
Danny the Deadleg was discovered
Done to death
By a dangerous, deluded desperado.

Dawn next day detectives
Deeply distressed
Duly declared Danny the Deadleg
Definitely dead on Deansgate
And described the dastardly dagger
That had done the
Despicable deed.

Kevin Cooper

HAPPY NEW YEAR

When the clock strikes 12
We all dance and cheer
Everyone shouting 'Happy New Year!'
The party never ends
With family and friends
Men drinking beer
We all shout and cheer
Glad to let in the new year.

Tracy Poynton

PLEASE

'Please feed me,' says the outstretched
hands of the child.
Her bowl is empty.
Her eyes are empty.
The guns are now still.
Whose greed did they fulfil?
Not mine - not yours.
But our voices still roar.
Only the child's silent approach can be heard.
Just one word.
'Please!'
'Please feed me,' says the outstretched
hands of the child.

Dawn Dalrymple

INDECISION

I don't know what to say,
I don't know what to do.
I'm so indecisive,
Oh, if I only knew.
I may decide tomorrow,
Or, possibly next week.
That elusive decision,
The conclusion I seek.

Self doubt is around me,
My confidence is low.
Keep that stiff upper lip,
Don't let the edges show.
Life is in the fast lane,
Who can I really trust.
Maybe my intuition,
Oh, if I really must.

K H Watts

THINK POSITIVE

So now I'm in my 80th year
How should I greet the day?
I've 80 years of knowledge
Picked up along life's way.

I go out walking every morn
And hold my head up high,
My stomach in my shoulders back
And smiles for passers by.

For did you know with every smile
The endomorphines flow.
They build up my immunity
And give an inner glow.

I never say 'I'll save my legs'
But do a journey twice
It gives me lots of exercise
Sometimes I do it thrice.

Last year I got out my old bike
To give my feet a rest,
My knees are now so flexible
I bend and stretch with zest.

Some folks are old at 42
And young at 90 odd,
Your age is just a state of mind
Not just how fast you plod.

This world is such a wondrous place
Enjoy it to the full.
Think positive and you will find
That life is never dull.

Jean Gray

THE DOORBELL IS RINGING

The doorbell is ringing, is it someone for me?
No, I don't think so,
There are people coming - perhaps it's for me.
No, I don't think so.
No, well I guess not. Well at least not today,
Perhaps, maybe tomorrow.
My mam, she said, she'd come back for me.
No, I don't think so.
I wait, and I wait, for the doorbell to ring,
Then I say,
Is it someone for me?
No, I don't think so,
Maybe just once.
It could be for me.
Is my mam coming?
Will anybody tell me the truth.
No, I don't think so.
Does anybody love me.
No, I don't think so.
Not today - maybe another day.
No, I don't think so.
Do I have to stay in this children's home.
Yes, yes I think so.

Janet Kelly

FRIENDS

Friends are precious all through life,
We couldn't be without them,
Someone to talk with through stress and strife,
Someone to share good times with.

For a start we share our toys,
Often we need persuading,
Then all our secrets, both sorrow and joys,
When childhood is rapidly fading.

We fall in love and tell our friend,
We're hit by 'Cupid's dart'
He meets another - it comes to an end,
Our friend helps to mend a broken heart.

Then comes the one who's friend and lover,
He wants you for his wife,
This sort of friendship lasts forever,
And brings joy to all of your life.

So never undervalue friends,
Life without them would be sad,
Young ones, old ones, all different kinds,
Giving help through times good and bad.

D M Carne

THE MARK OF HONOUR

A little lady, sits and stares,
It maybe that she says her prayers.
Yet wonder I, what she thinks,
It maybe colours, pretty pinks.

Yet stares she through, her window lost,
It maybe, she counts the cost.
Or sees the hills, so far away,
And think it is, a lovely day.

Or wonders, when her end will be,
Thinks soon, that God, will set her free.
And memories of days gone by,
That brings a tear, within her eye.

Remembers, when she was a child,
And her mother, meek and mild.
She drowses gently into sleep,
Her precious memories, kept in keep.

Thinks of children, growing up,
Or when they bought a little pup.
And sad moments, when they left,
A stabbing pain, that leaves a cleft.

An empty echo, that's left behind,
The husband she loved, that was so kind.
The sorrow she felt, when he was gone,
Of the struggle, it was, to carry on.

Marks of courage, printed deep on her face,
A medal of honour, that bears no disgrace.
Think softly, deep within my soul,
Will I one day, be half so whole.

Mary Gore

FEELINGS

Feelings are weird, feelings are strange,
Feelings come in a very wide range.
Feelings are like a mountain range,
Feelings can make people change.

Feelings are very weird,
Feelings need caution whenever neared.
Feelings are like a long grey beard,
Feelings are something to be feared.

Feelings are really great,
Feelings give us love and hate.
Feelings really are first rate,
Feelings can decide our fate.

Tom Syron (13)

BYGONE DAYS

Do you often sit back - think and recall
Of the old memories, passed by us all
Those days of 'black pudding' and 'blackberry pie'
Milk from the farms, you always could buy.

The vegetable plots in our garden we grew
Fresh daily produce - 'twas so healthy for you
The 'brawn' on the thrall, and dripping to eat
Home-made jam was a real special treat

Monday was always - 'the washing day'
Mangled by hand, hard work you could say
Cooking for many, a chore done by most
Whether it 'hot pot' or plain piece of toast

Carbolic soap, for that refreshing scrub
The old kettle boiling to add to the tub
Sharing the water with one another
Little sister maybe - or could be 'big brother'

Though times were hard, we had so much fun
Helping each other till all work was done
Large families we had - so loving and giving
Toiling and striving, but that was hard living

Our boots we would polish, till they did shine
A 'tanner' a week, that's all that was mine
Yet the happiness found - with just a few pence
Is a treat to remember, the good old days 'hence'.

Veronica Buckby

A SPRING SONNET

The scents of spring pervade the air
Enchanting senses everywhere.
A walk through woods uplifts the heart
With bluebells spread their joys impart.
Hidden in branches from our sight
Birds sing out for our delight.
The cherry blossom off the trees
Falls like confetti in the breeze.
Shy violets in hedgerow found
But ladysmocks in fields abound.
Gone the cold and snow so drear
Hope fills the soul new life is here.
Rejoice! Rejoice! Let earth resound
All nature cries with one glad sound.

Beryl M Malkin

BORROWED TIME

Autumn leaves bade farewell
To the trees they have adorned so well.

The proud trees stood with all their colours
Now all hopes dashed by autumn weather.

The leaves now blow about in piles
Telling us that winter's nigh.

They'll come again another spring
New hope to all of us will bring.

It's the same in human life you see
New babies to replace you and me.

Nothing or nobody lasts forever
It has to be replaced.

Keith Wilson

THE END OF THE WORLD

The wind howls, the rain pours down,
Alone I stand, draped in a satin gown.
In the middle of nowhere, completely lost,
My hair now a mess, crumpled and tossed.

Trees bend over, leaves cover my eyes,
The dust from the earth begins to rise.
I'm so scared, I'm all alone,
The bitter wind continues to moan.

Slowly my eyes catch a glimpse of the sky,
The man in the moon seems to whisper goodbye.
All of the stars start to drift away,
It must be the beginning of another new day.

Yet I am wrong, as the sun doesn't appear,
And total darkness seems inevitably near.
Suddenly I realise what's going on,
Soon everything around me will all be gone.

And now I stand, alone in the dark,
History now will make its mark.
The world's going to end, I will stand bereft,
Of people and places, I'll be the only thing left.

As reality finally begins to sink in,
My tears of pain slowly begin.
Now at breaking point, I struggle to call,
It's completely useless, I allow myself to fall.

As I start to fall, I see my life pass me by,
I pray to God that I too will die.
Nothing remains but my echoing scream,
As I wake up and realise it was a dream.

Laura Murray

A LAND BECKONING

The Highlands are calling me
  O'er mountains and glens,
Come to my lonely crags
  With their wild flowering scents.

Kind faces will welcome me
  In shielings by the shore,
Where golden sands beckon
  And the winged seagulls soar.

Oh for the grand view
  Of dark Lochnagar
With a glimpse of an eagle
  On that summit so far.

Take me in darkness
  In sunshine or flood,
In any Scot's weather
  I'll be stirred in the blood.

Jim Carnduff

TIME STOOD STILL

Time stood still,
I had no will,
To see things through.

Time stood still,
People on the move,
Nothing left to prove.

Time stood still,
Nowhere left to go,
Just wanting to scream 'No!'

Time stood still,
I had to stand back and evaluate,
What my life would now mean I couldn't speculate.

Time stood still,
Running water still running,
But to my friends only shunning.

Time stood still,
Was it only my time,
Why did the clock still chime?

Time stood still,
Walking slowly up a hill,
No control over my own will.

Time stood still the day he died,
Just let me go and run and hide.
The biggest piece of my heart has gone away.
Please don't leave me in this place, I don't want to stay.

J Sweet

THE RIDDLE OF LIFE

Together, we stand alone.
Sadness, hurt, and lingering pain.
The heartache comes to many,
But remembered lovingly with a smile.
Can we solve the 'riddle of our life in time'?

No more their whispered words we hear,
Just memories and dreams untold.
Gone is their gentle touch,
Their friendship we once shared.
Can we ever *solve* the 'riddle of our life in time'?

Jean M Stevens

ALWAYS

Always be sincere,
And good devoted, patient too,
Don't hound yourself with too much pride
Or have revenge take you . . .

Always have a warm, kind hand
And share with those in need,
And always keep in sympathy
Afflicted hearts that bleed!

Always keep a joyful heart
And hope do keep with you,
And always unto others do
Love as you love you . . .

Never curse nor harbour hate,
Don't burden you this fate,
But keep a mind of goodness
In its perfect happy state.

A Rothwell

INSPIRATIONS

I started writing poetry
A year or so ago
When I was feeling down
And at an all time low

God inspired me to write these words
But I didn't know where to start
But if you ever read them
You'll know there from my heart

So when m y work is published
I'm sure you will agree
My poetry is quite unique
Written just by me

P A Williams

NOTHING

The hot sun in the sky
The warm wind through the trees
But now there's just darkness
Not even a breeze.

A young orphan boy
Screams and cries for his mum
But there's no sounds, there's no teardrops
Cause he's blind, deaf and dumb.

He reaches out in vain
For a mum who's not there
There is no one to love him
There's no one to care.

An old woman struggles to carry her shopping
But her bag just holds teardrops
No groceries, no nothing.

She stoops to keep warm
By an unlit fire
Her thoughts turn to yesterday
Of love and desire.

She keeps all her memories
In an old tin box
Which cannot be opened
There's no key, there's no lock just nothing.

Elizabeth Ann Hull

BIG MOVIES

The dialogue is sharp in the classic Big Sleep
But the plot complications do go a bit deep.

The Big Clock is ticking to find out who is
The murderous one in the publishing biz.

It's The Big Heat and poor Gloria's got
Her one cup of coffee a little too hot!

The Marx Brothers loose in the funny Big Store
Can only leave you with a glow, wanting more.

The Big Circus gives us spectacular fun
But walking the tightrope's not easily done.

The silent greatness of The Big Parade
Its anti-war message will never fade.

Rooney's the driver behind The Big Wheel
We know he'll come god in the burning last reel.

Stick The Big Knife in and don't blink an eye
The Hollywood way is the best way to die!

The Big Country where emotions soar
To Jerome Moross's epic sore.

Along the Missouri to where dangers lurk
Across The Big Sky starring fur-trapped, Kirk.

The Big Boodle gamblers, their luck didn't last
And Errol's done much better films in the past.

The twisting plot of The Big Steal
For Mitchum's Army payroll deal.

The Big Combo's a thriller directed with style
And Wilde knew that Conte was bad all the while.

Big Trouble in Little China chop-suey
Is a load of Oriental kung-fuey!

The Big Trail, Big Jake and Big Jim McLain
All of these movies starred big man, John Wayne.

Cavan Magner

HOLIDAYS

Holiday time is drawing near,
Where are we going to go this year?
Somewhere nice, so warm and sunny,
Lots to do, take plenty of money.
Lists are made and clothing bought,
Plenty of sunscreen, it could be hot.
Cases are empty and ready to pack,
Two weeks later and it's time to come back.

J Cameron

THE VALLEY OF THE KINGS

Outside, a bustling city lies
The traffic's rumble, children's cries
A million tourists' moving feet
Through the desert's dusty heat
Time will not touch the ageless faces
Of those who slept within these places
Our busy world has passed them by
They saw not death, they saw the sky
Between these hills to wait together
They knew not death, they know forever
The fading pictures on the stone
Of kings who do not sleep alone
Their sleep of ages just a pause
In this place, no effect or cause
Millennia passed, but a moment gone
They belong to the stars, the many are one.

Alma Cooper

DAD

Battered old grey trilby stained with years of wear,
I remember it so clearly, hiding the thick grey hair.
Brown baggy trousers hanging from a waist nipped with age,
A grubby blue shirt, left unbuttoned when he was in a rage.
His favourite tie hung round his neck,
Covered in last night's tea.
Oh how these clothes bring fond memories back to me.
His walking stick lies idling, his pipe gnarled and decayed,
One tatty shoe is cast aside with its laces frayed.
Goodness only knows for how long these clothes he had,
But when I see them around, I think of my dear old dad.

Josie Rawson

THE TRAVELLER

O light thou traveller from the east
Depart not swiftly on thy way
Put up thy caravan and feast
And sport with me awhile I pray

The long night hours have slowly died
I welcome thee, o stay awhile
Shed thy bright beams where nought can hide
And my whole being greet thy smile

Thy rays invincible hath power
To paint the clouds with flame and rose
All nature is thy living dower
As darkness on its journey goes

Like life thy hours are free to all
Love and enjoy them to the last
For when the sombre curtains fall
The joy and inclination's past

M Eccleston

MY GUARDIAN ANGELS

I am very lucky you know, some people are lucky and have one
guardian angel, I have two!
They are both contrasts of each other, yet they join perfectly as one
golden star,
Which shines so bright across heaven it simply lifts your soul.
Each comforts me in a different way, but they comfort my sores no
less or more than each other.
One is female, her name is selfless, generous, understanding,
loving angel.
We work on the same level and she knows my thoughts,
sometimes even before I.
Her smile penetrates my darkest hours, and her painful tears
roll down my cheeks.
I watch each graceful step she takes, hoping I too will follow in her
loving travels.
The other is male, his name is strong, wise, eternally giving,
loving angel.
He is strong and his steps put pride in my twinkling, admiring eyes.
I know that he will do anything to protect me and I always feel warm
in my cloud blanket.
I wish for just one ounce of his courage and wisdom.
I love both my guardian angels with every part of my little heart,
but it is not enough.
To them I am eternally grateful, I could never fly as they do.
Their wings are made of silver and their hearts of gold.
I could never sing the beautiful notes that they deserve to be sung,
But to them I offer myself, I'll continue to learn and hopefully go on
to teach what I have learnt.
They do not hear the words often enough, but I whisper softly from
the bottom of my heart,
I truly love my guardian angels.
May they always be safe, they will always be held in my loved heart.

Deanne Edwards

APRIL MORN

On this April morn
      the sun is shining bright,
A little bit of cheer
      to make everything seem right.
I put away my cares
      just for a little while,
It seems Mother Nature
      is giving out a smile.
The glory in the garden
      with daffodils in bloom,
Tell of summer's hopes
      goodbye to winter's gloom.
They seem to gaily wave
      then nod their heads to me,
Standing there so proudly
      dancing in their glee.
I gaze upon these golden flowers
      whose beauty is unshorn,
Giving out their message
      of life once more reborn.

G F Green

SOUNDS

Bells ringing
Birds singing
Bubbles popping
Bunnies hopping
Frogs jumping
Music pumping
People talking
Quacking gosling
Owls hooting
Hunters shooting
Teeth crunching
Children munching
Water running
Trains coming
Baby crying
Mother sighing

Lindsey Knowles

BE YOU

Love will bring you acceptance,
No constant struggling to please,
Differences hold no importance,
A sanctuary, a haven, a release.

At ease with a comfortable silence,
Content when conversation flows,
No need for falsehoods or pretence,
When your loyalty strengthens and grows.

Once sealed the bonds won't be broken,
Though wear may occur at the seam,
A kind gesture or a small token,
Will reinforce a true winning team.

On offer to all, just remember,
Not only the privileged few,
A lover, friend or family member,
With whoever you can simply be you.

M O'Driscoll

FROM A HOSPITAL BED

I waited on a call from you
To say 'Hello' to me
As you were of the chosen 'few'
When I was young and free.

But oh alas 'twas not to hear
The sweet melodious tone
Of the 'Nightingale' from yonder year
Above the traffic drone.

So I languished day by day
The nights were dark and long
When there upon my back I lay
I heard a warbling song.

Just outside the windowpane
A blackbird and her mate
Were sitting in the pouring rain
Atop a garden gate.

Hello, hello my ancient friend
You won't be sick for long
We can see you're on the mend
Lay back, enjoy our song!

And oh so pure the tunes of love
From each smooth, shiny throat
It was as if a turtle dove
Had penned each tiny note.

Perhaps it was the Lord on high
Oh this His Easter morn
Who sent these pilgrims from the sky
To herald in the dawn.

And then 'twas done
The thread was broke
The birds had flown away
The rain had stopped
The sun was out
T'would be a brilliant day!

JAT (Paddy)

CHRISTMAS 1936

What is that thing in the corner Daddy
That you have got for Christmas this year
It's black with glass in the middle Daddy
Its purpose I know not I fear

Child - that thing will change us forever
We shan't need to read or converse
We need not play games again ever
Our pleasures will not be diverse

It will control our lives completely
We shall watch it night and day long
It resides by the fire so neatly
Replacing both music and song

What is its purpose? Do we just look
And what does the stupid thing do?
All is revealed in the handbook
Which we must completely read through

First insert plug into socket
Electric supply to obtain
But Dad, we don't have a socket
Or even a wired ring main

It won't work on candles or coal gas
This thing without reason or rhyme
Daughter I fear I've been conned lass
It's many years before its time

At least we can talk to each other
Our problems we each shall console
Without any fighting or bother
Over who holds the remote control

John Crick

LIGHT BEYOND THE DARKNESS

November's dismal wet weather,
Claustrophobic, so limiting,
An overcast sky, no measure
Of brightness, so dispiriting.
And still dark thoughts invade my mind,
Recalling how a friend would end
His life; when shock subsides, we find
Not the imbalance in our friend,
Whose sharper clarity of mind,
Might put the smuggest judge to shame,
But a planned journey, that should bind
Us to acceptance, without blame.
Now an uncurtained wintry sun
Through the glass upon my shoulders,
Loosens the band of weariness,
Depression no longer smoulders.
Savouring the warmth of a log
Burning fire, intoxicated,
Surrounded by books, safe from fog,
Contentment - not overstated.

Alexander Winter

CLOSING MY EYES

Why must I live
Why can't I die
Why must I live this awful lie
Living daily in this life
So full of sorrow, full of strife
Why can't I simply go to sleep
Why must this troubled life I keep
Why does my sadness lie so deep
Why can't I take my final breath and slip unnoticed into death?

Why should I smile, say all is well
Whilst treading living boards of hell
Why can't the truth I bravely tell
Why must I wait for the final bell
Why should I keep normality
Pretending false vitality
Protecting my humanity
Is ruining my sanity
Why can't I take my final breath and slip unnoticed into death?

Why can't the final act I close
I am a coward I suppose
I cannot form the ending prose
Why can't I break this ancient law
To drift in sleep for evermore
Why must I live, each day I pray
That I shan't see another day
I cannot find another way
Why can't I take my final breath and slip unnoticed into death?

When will I close my eyes to sleep
My passing marked with sombre wreath
Why must this life span time so long
Why does it just go on and on, when will this hell on earth be done?

Patricia Berwick

WOUNDED HEART

You broke my heart in two the day
You packed your bags and went away.

And I could not believe it when
You came back, to do it all again.

I cried and screamed and fell apart
But you must have a wooden heart.

I made mistakes myself I know
But you just did not have to go.

When darkness falls I think of you
Convince myself that you do to.

Because the truth's too much too bear
How can I think that you don't care?

My biggest wish would be for you
To see yourself as others do.

When you're a mum yourself you'll know
Just how much I love you so.

Sandra Sherratt

FISHERMAN'S FOLLY

Two men did leave the shore one day,
There was a force five blowing.
They had never fished the sea before,
And didn't know where they where going.

An old salt saw the stormy weather,
And warned them not to go,
For he had lived there all his life,
And he should surely know.

But alas for them the fool hardy ones,
They did not heed his wish.
Instead of which they set a course,
And went to seek the fish.

No flares or lifejackets did they carry,
Or torch to tell of their plight.
And people on the shore did worry,
When they failed to return that night.

The lifeboat it did put to sea,
And searched the sea till dusk.
If only they had had a flare,
It really is a must.

Neither men or boat were seen again,
So if you put to sea,
Remember all the safety gear,
And you will be home for tea.

Jim Mankelow

MY LITTLE GIRL

My little girl,
With eyes that smile,
That makes me fill up with pride,
You who needed me as a child,
As I need you to help me survive,
All your strength and all your weaknesses,
Brings to me - my own defeats.

Being near you, I feel warm,
Never cold or forlorn,
Oh daughter you won't understand,
What joy I feel that you are mine,
You're everything I could ever wish,
And more inside a loving kiss.

Oh daughter you are my pride and joy,
Watching you grow,
More inside with a heart,
And feelings that understands,
You are more to me than me.

When I'm gone sing a song,
Don't be sad and drag on,
Of my life I've had a good one.

To Cara, love always Mum.

C McGrath

A POET IN A MESS

At last has come my chance to write
A rhyme to put in print.
Are fame and fortune in my sight,
Shall I soon make a mint?
If I should have the chance to climb
The ladder of success
I'm sure that it would be sublime
but don't I look a mess.
Perhaps the time has now arrived
When I must start my diet,
Over many years I have strived,
to grill my food, not fry it.
I've cycled, exercised and ran,
But nothing alters me.
So I'll be famous if I can
Just keep me off TV.

Dawn Murray

THANK GOD IT'S MONDAY

The alarm clock thunders inside my head
Oh how I wish I could stay in bed
It's Monday morning yet again
Another week of misery and pain
I get up and comb my hair
And wonder if I really care

I can see pictures inside my head
Of friends I've lost or are now dead
There's no one here to comfort me
And if there was they wouldn't see
If there is a better life after death
Then please God take me to your breast

Maybe today won't be like the rest
I've decided it's to be the best
The smell of gas doesn't bother me
So now my body must lay to rest
Monday's aren't so bad at all
In fact they're the best of all

Venus Wakley

To Halina.
For Your New Home

Hope that you'll be happy -
You deserve to be,
Let your cheerful goodness flow
In whatever place you see,
Not forgetting either,
All you've done for me.

Keep your spontaneity,
One of life's great gifts;
Sense of humour, you've that too
Calming down the rifts;
In your new home may there be
Kindness, love, serenity.

Laurie Green

LOVE'S SURPRISE

I love you very much
and
my heart is taking charge.
It matters not the sense of it.
Or if you should feel the same.
I didn't need to fall in love,
It was never planned.
More reasons not to - you'll agree,
But proving love is blind!

Maureen Hooper

My Cottage Of The Winds

I tarried wrong for far too long
In search of better years
With yearnings for encouragement
But still I'm sitting here
And still I dream of cliff top's greens
With sunlight breaking in
To warm my heart and soul
Within my cottage of the winds
A dappling tapestry of gold
That dances through the leaves
Of oak trees swaying softly
In a silent summer breeze
For no more life could offer me
My everything it seems
I hear it call each waking hour
And see it in my dreams
Curse this concrete jungle
Curse its cold sadistic sins
That keeps me from my home, which is
My cottage of the winds

Ken Watson

GRANDFATHER TAUGHT ME

Tell me Grandfather, of the riches of this land,
Teach me how to paint, like your fine hand.
Teach me of the seasons that are three months apart,
So I like you, can capture the feelings in my heart.

First told by teachers, which were half understood,
To believe their tales, I never could.
Telling us of the future, which were total lies,
Making us believe that we live, then just die.

Teach me Grandfather, what I see in your eyes,
The romance of England's beauty, where your soul lies.
Show me where the moss grows silky green,
Teach me of the breathing land and your sights of Eden.

L E Richmond

SECRETS

I never would reveal
The feelings that I feel

I never would tell out
The things I'm told about

I never would unfold
The secrets I've been told

No matter what I've heard
I wouldn't say a word

The confidence you said
Lays deep inside and dead

Once told, I'd never tell
Or I would burn in Hell!

Danny Miller

IF YOU DON'T ENTER YOU WON'T WIN!

On Saturday the ninth, we have the village show
And one member entered several things, I thought you'd like to know.
Her name is Mavis Gardener and in vegetables and fruit
She's put in five potatoes and they've all come off one root,
And in the flower section eighteen inches overall,
She's been inspired by Nature with an arrangement proud and tall.
The home-made has come easy, she really likes to bake,
The loaf is brown, the jam is sweet, and oh, her chocolate cake.
At art and craft she too excels, her needlework astounds,
Mave's even done a two-in-one, a toy, with lacework all around.
She took pics of ancient buildings and one looking out to sea
And even produced a birthday card with words to you from me.
She's tried to enter every class, she wants the show to stay
And if it is she doesn't win, well who cares anyway.
She knows her pears aren't good enough,
And how are onions dressed?
The wasps enjoyed her apples and her dahlias full of pest.
Her cucumber is curly and she hasn't got a truss,
But I hope she wins on Saturday,
Mave could be one of us.

Gill Roach

THE WARRIOR

He stands strongly - at the edge of his land
A warrior - noble, unafraid of invading forces.
Those that would take away his gains
Never would he let an inch go.

He moves quickly - enemies come near,
Move to strike at his home
From the air, from the ground, all around
Never would he let an inch go.

He fights bravely - the odds are impossible
His foes, pained from his attack, push harder
The pace quickens 'til all battle is blurred.
Never would he let an inch go.

He wills firmly the tide of fate to turn his way,
War fades, the conqueror keeps his spoils.
Our robin red breast gleaming, on his bird table,
Never, never, *never* would he let an inch go.

Sue Cotterell

NIGHTMARE

I walked through the cemetery, so cold and bare
Thinking that no other person was there.
Coming towards me, two youths and a man
The threatening gleam of a blade in his hand.
I held my head high, just try if he dare
And swiftly walked past, as if they weren't there.
But I was wrong, to my sorrow I found
The blade in my neck, and my body to ground
With growing anger I rose to my feet
They stood there looking, white as a sheet.
I suddenly started to rise in the air
A voice deep within me, like wails of despair
I hovered above them, they scattered like sheep
My husband was shaking me out of my sleep
'Wake up! You're having a bad dream' he said.
'The noise you were making, could waken the dead.'

Jean Birch

A Dog Came Into My Life

Never again we said in pain,
But our cries were in vain.
Our last dog departing sadly
Left us feeling bereft badly.

Now into our lives you came,
More than willing for a game.
Tall and big you grew,
But docile, to give you your due.

Naughty at times, as you dig,
Maybe this is because you're so big.
Yet love you do show
And behind me you move in tow.

I'm so glad you came into our life
Because we'd been through such strife,
Now you do make me smile
Even though I've to run after you a mile.

So much love to us you give,
Now with us that you live.
When a little sad do I feel,
Then my heart you do steal.

Your snout do touch my hand,
With a tongue that feels like sand.
'Be happy,' you try to say
Keep all your sorrows at bay.

Susan Shaw

MY TEMPERAMENTAL AUTO

My Ford is my transport.
I have no other
To last me a lifetime
No chance for another.
It starts in the morning
On bright sunny days.
But won't face the music
On cold frosty days.

It stands in the driveway gleaming
All bright and very shiny.
But the mood it's in, I have to say.
It's failed to start again today
It bucks and jumps and gives a sigh.
It's a sod this morning the neighbours cry.

It will not get the better of me
I'll try again after a cup of tea.
I press the starter with trepidation.
It backfires and bangs in consternation
And upsets the dogs in all creation.

I try again and creep upon it
And listen closely 'neath the bonnet.
I think I hear a familiar sound
As I put my ear close to the ground
It's ticking over quite merrily
It must have been that cup of tea.

A Bennett

I DREAM FOR YOU

Chill me to the bone
And tell me what you know.
Take me to the places
You know I long to go.

Get me through the night
Without that sense of ache.
Take me to the pillow,
Never let me wake.

Let the journey back
Be silent, calm and true.
Do it all over again
Till I fall in love with you.

Helen Cattle

FLOODS

Rain, falls down,
Slowly, softly at first,
Caressing, the plants and hedges,
Fingering the cars.
Feeling its way around the buildings and walls,
Embracing all the people, while,
Umbrellas go up to shield.
Hand in hand with the wind,
Suddenly the clouds give a roar,
A fiery rage,
A storm erupts.
Gusty, raging, furious the rain,
Forcing away everything in its path.
Filling up the roads,
The drains are blocked,
The rivers overflow.
Uninvited into people's homes.
Battling with sand bags placed to protect,
Refusing to give up, determined on destroying.
Days and weeks of misery and despair.
Then it all ends, the sun breaks through.
It's time to rebuild and repair,
Until the next time.

Robina Perveen Khan

THE DIFFERENCE BETWEEN MEN AND WOMEN

The difference between men and women,
Is really easy to see,
We sit down and you stand up,
That's how we differ to pee.

The art of making a cuppa,
Is not in your nature to do,
You simply can't co-ordinate,
So it can't be left up to you.

Decision making that's what you do best,
Or at least that's what you think,
You whiz around in your own little world,
But you've forgotten where's the sink.

Your dirty washing seems to collect,
But never in one place,
I don't think you know what a washing machine is,
By that blank look on your face.

You make the place look untidy,
You've got it down to an art,
You wolf down all your dinner,
Even before I've made a start.

Half a conversation,
That's all you manage to take in,
But if you were the perfect man,
I would probably be as miserable as sin.

We all have these faults you see,
You can't help being a man,
It's one of the things I have to live with,
And I make the best I can.

S Wood

THE VORTEX

The breeze was cool and calm,
The sea stood motionless as a rock,
The sun shone brightly
As men stood from the dock.

Dark clouds crept over the sea
As sunlight faded away,
Wind began to howl and moan
As trees on shore began to sway.

Dark clouds began to circle the sea.
As the sea began to rise high,
Giving out a huge roar, like a ferocious beast
As a tornado suddenly appeared from the sky.

The tornado tore through the sea
Twisting its long funnel of raging power,
Spraying water everywhere,
As the tornado will reach land in a matter of hours.

As the sea grew more vicious
Rain as sharp as spears
Falling from the darkness above,
The islanders facing their worst fears.

Winds began to slowly cease,
The tornado began to slowly die
As darks clouds fading away,
The sun lighting up the sky.

The islanders are safe for now,
But it will be back
It might be shining brightly
But again, the sky will soon turn black.

Gwen Smullen

PLAY WITH CARE

Playing Frisbee
To and fro
Back and forth
Tossed high out of reach
Away from the beach
Over sea
And lands
On the waves
Down
Down
Down
Down
Around, turning, twisting,
        avoiding obstacles,
Fish and barnacles
Wrecks and oysters
Gone.

Elaine Lovegrove

JADED

A bomb went off in the streets today,
I'm not afraid it happens everyday,
It killed two men, a mother and child
She was actually nursing she looked so mild.
But when it was over I couldn't see her face
It had been torn off, from crown to base.
It made me sad to think the baby was dead
It was a cute little thing who never cried in bed
Apart from that I'm not even riled
Don't think me ignorant, I'm not a child
But bombs go off everyday in our streets you see,
And if I wept each time then where would I be?
There's a war going on in my country again,
Someone wants to rule, oh I forget his name
Is it Taylor, or Kabila, or Seseseko?
Well, whatever it is, what's one to do?
I'm waiting for the UN they're bringing us aid
And if Kofi is smart soon I'll be drinking lemonade
And living my life without a care
As I was before, before my soul was stripped bare.

Sope Williams

MY CHILDREN

I'll never forget my firstborn, it was 3.56pm,
She was 7lb 4oz with big blue eyes,
Masses of hair and a dimpled chin,
The most beautiful face you have ever seen,
It was worth all the pain and the mess and the fuss,
This little baby was part of us,
I held her close, though she was still in a mess,
And her instincts led her straight to my breast,
The most incredible feeling filled my heart,
As she suckled hungrily from the start,
I slipped into sleep when they took her away,
And dreamt of a future so rosy,
Then they brought her back all clean and fresh,
And wrapped up nice and cosy,
That gift of a child was mine to hold,
To love and care for forever,
I felt so proud she was part of me.
That feeling I'll always treasure.

Her blue eyes turned brown my world turned upside down,
My house was full of nappies, in buckets, in sinks,
This bathroom stinks, would I ever again be happy?
My night's sleep went bang, swapped for pushing a pram,
For topping and tailing and hours of wailing,
For bonnets and booties and furry cuties,
Short night and short tempers, so we changed to Pampers,
The washing was cut by a mile, but so was the cash,
They end up in the trash, so back to Terries for a while.
Then it was teething, my god that screaming went on for evermore,
The first tooth came through, then there were two,
My poor baby's mouth was so sore, but so was my head,
How I needed my bed, which is when I announced 'No more',
Never again would I suffer this pain,
She's 12 now, one's 8 and one's 4.

Marie Lee

LIFE . . .

A loose grip on life is what you've been given,
pushed into a hard world to live in.
Hurdles to cross from day to day,
objects always distracting your way.
A freedom of speech is what they state,
but whoever listens it's always too late.
Work, who made that up must of been mad,
but maybe their life was also so sad.
A world full of hate, a world of crime,
it's hard to live in this present time.
It's not even safe to walk down a street,
always weary of the people you could meet.
Like one big queue, always having a wait,
then who's the person who decides your fate.
Don't get me wrong, it's not all doom and gloom,
when happiness creeps in and begins to bloom.
Then life sort of becomes a high,
with your body so light you could even fly.
Then that's when things are such a blast,
really not knowing how long it would last.
Making mistakes might help you learn,
there's still always something more you yearn.
Then all of a sudden it comes to a stop,
once again, it's one big flop.
You ask why? Whatever went wrong,
how will you cope, will you get along.
So tell me the person, the one to blame,
of making your life, how it became.

Michelle Duffy

A SOLDIER'S PRAYER

As dawn breaks with slashing rain, I lay here in the mud.
And think of home, of pastures green, and not of all the blood.
The blood of friends and foes alike, who lay here in this field,
I ask the Lord for strength of heart, and pray for those I've killed.
A single tear rolls down my face, for death has come for me.
I pray my wife will tell my son, a son I'll never see.
His father died with strength and courage, for Country, God and King,
And when this war is long since past, let sons and daughters sing,
The praises of the souls lost her in battlefields of mud,
So that the world could live in peace, your fathers gave their blood.

Ryan Goldsmith

ON THE ROAD TO GARDA

On the road to Garda
    from Calais down through France
Across the Strasbourg border
    thro' Switzerland we pass - and
All those mighty mountains - high
    in the Italian Alps - with
Miles and miles of vineyards everywhere

Along the road to Riva - a -
    round the shores we roam - with
Miles of market street stalls
    selling many things - unknown
Windows full of flowers
    everywhere we go - and
Everyone's on holiday - like you!

A magic trip to Venice
    a city full of dreams - a
Coffee in St Mark's Square - a
    must - to be seen!
Beneath the Bridge of Sighs - a
    romantic trip in a gondola!
Recalls a song about a -
    famous Cornetto!

Staying at Torbole - our
    holiday hotel - and
Strolling by the lakeside - in
    the cool evening air
All those mighty mountains -
    reflected everywhere -
Holiday to remember - at
    our holiday hotel!

Nelson

REFLECTION

The greatest things in life
Are the ones we overlook
The ones we take for granted
The liberties we took

But the portents we are given
Are ignored, cos we are fools
Can we really be so selfish
Or are we stubborn mules

One thing we can be sure on
If our ways we do not mend
Hell is our destination
Could it really be, the end?

Anthony D Beardsley

STRAWBERRY VALLEY

I look back at those days, with nostalgic sighs,
As I get older, the time really flies,
So come my friend, come with me,
Back to where, our memories be,

Let's climb above the splendour, of the streets we once knew,
Where most have all gone, they've only left a few,
Let's search for the sights and the sounds, that are there in our minds,
Come with me my friend, let's see what we can find,

We'll go back to the friendliest people, you could ever meet,
In the old terraced houses, street after street,
With streets full of children, all playing their games,
And such friendly neighbours, remember their names,

There was 'Hynam', and 'Eynon', 'Cleavey' and 'Keach',
Just some of the names, that lived in our street,
Remember then the old lower road,
With 'Jenkins', 'Haywood' and 'Price',
Who would stick together, through thick and thin,
They were oh so friendly and nice,

Yes, my friend, we'll remember and behold,
The steam from those engines of old,
Where they pilfered the coal, from the wagons,
To keep warm, and protect them, from the cold,

Where women would linger, fags all alight,
And old men wore 'dai-caps', from morning till night,
With shifting curtains, and shadows just gone,
Searching for gossip, that they could pass on,

But emerging my friend, is a new lower road,
Let's hope it will shape, with the same friendly code,
Where people will pull together and rally,
The second time around, in our 'Strawberry Valley'.

Bill Gabb

SLOW TO LEARN

They've got me down as 'slow to learn'
But I can really do quite a lot,
I know the radiators my hands can burn,
And if you put me on the spot,
I can shout for Mum, and take off my shoes,
And climb the table too.
I know to use my blanket, so my head I do not bruise.

When you tell me not to do it, I understand every word,
So to say that I am slow to learn, is really quite absurd.
If you ask me if I want some cake, I nod and say 'yes'
That's fine,
I understand your language, can I help it if you don't
Know mine?

So don't put me down as slow to learn,
It really isn't true,
It's you that has a lot to learn, 'cause I can
Understand you.

Joy Moss

THE QUIZ NIGHT

A quiz night's been arranged for us,
We've polished our brains, we're all a-buzz,
But first of all, we've got to eat
A fish and chip supper, what a treat,
Now all settle down, this is serious stuff.
First form into 3's without too much fuss,
Now choose a leader, one who can write,
Don't worry about spellings, so long as it's right:
'Who opened this place? Was it a he or a she?
It's there on a plaque for all to see,'
Who was it who said, 'Hello, and welcome?'
You can fair hear our brains as they sizzle and burn,
What a wonderful thing a memory is,
We had one once, now it's given us a miss,
Who sang, 'Release me, let me go?'
Tom what's his name, someone must know.
'The Ponderosa,' she said, now let us see,
Why that was Bonanza we whisper with glee,
Here's another question, our minds have gone blank,
We've just got to admit it, we're as thick as two planks.
If I were a politician with the gift of the gab,
I would urge my team on with professional blab,
'Who talked to the animals?' Our minds are so fickle,
Of course we know that, it was Dr Dolittle,
It's over at last, we've done of our best,
Our minds have certainly been put to the test,
What does it matter if we haven't won?
Let's do it again, it's really been fun.

Mary Smith

MY COPPER TREE

In the playground I planted this tiny tree.
It was a gift my headmaster bestowed on me.
I watched it grow day by day.
Then I grew up and went away.
But on my return there to my surprise.
Those copper leaves were touching the skies.
Around its base coiled a rustic seat.
Oh that fresh mown grass smelt just so sweet.
As I sat and drifted way back in time.
Oh those childhood years were indeed sublime.

T C Cronin

FAMILY BOND

I miss you all so very much
I feel that we are losing touch
The many miles between us now
Bring saddened furrows to my brow

I often look at a photograph
And remember how we used to laugh
We'd laugh at all that fate could bring
From tragedy to silly things

I raise a smile, but shed a tear
And all because you are not here
Of you, no one could be more fond
But then, that is our family bond

We know where to turn if a problem appears
Our strength has grown throughout the years
Though now we're apart, our bond's still there
Let no one dispute it, they wouldn't dare!

Frances Graves

THE TOTAL ECLIPSE

Off The Canadian coast at ten thirty
Was the start of the total eclipse
A thirty mile shadow across
As it raced past aircraft and ships

At two thousand miles per hour
It headed towards our south west
To Cornwall, Dorset and Devon
No good going there for a rest

It rained and it drizzled all morning
We hoped that the grey sky would clear
We had a few glimpses of sunshine
But the blue sky would not reappear

The day was the 11th of August
The year was nineteen nine nine
Eleven eleven was the hour
Sipping the celebration wine

We were saved from a total disaster
The media had hired a plane
To film the eclipse from a clear sky
And their efforts had not been in vain

They showed us some wonderful pictures
So clear all the way through
The darkness was eerie and awesome
Special glasses were needed to view

The peak of eclipse was Romania
The shadow was 70 miles wide
Travelling at 1500 miles per hour
To Iran on the western side

Baluchistan and on to Karachi
It will end as the sunset will fall
The moon's shadow is nearly over
As it reaches the Bay of Bengal.

Tom Rutherford

GROWING PAINS IN BELFAST

I'm fifteen years a boy now
In Belfast born and bred
And I fear like many friends of mine,
I may soon end up dead.

Will I grow up
Or be blown up
Will I be taken in my prime,
Will I make it through to manhood
Or die before my time

Will my family
See me flourish
And sire some children of my own
Or will they soon be mourning
As my name is cast in stone.

Is our home a safer haven
For my father after work,
When no one knows the enemy
Or when the dangers lurk

Will my mother be a widow
Before this year is passed
Can she be spared the agony
Or is the dye already cast.

Will my sister be unscathed
Or will she lose her life
Before the world sees sense
And puts an end to all this strife.

If I live to know the answers
I'll add more verses to this rhyme
But will you my friends
Complete these words
If I die before my time.

Bob Chadwick

PRICELESS THINGS

Looking down from the brow of the hill
Gazing over the lea
The plain, but wondrous sights, made by our Lord
Stretch forth, for all to see

The grass, swaying in the wind
The leaves rustling in the breeze
Like a giant ocean
Like waves upon the seas

Birds in the hedgerows singing their songs
Lambs in the meadows play
The river, running silently
As it flows upon its way

To see the colours, to hear the sounds
How fortunate we are
And when day turns into night, to look heavenward
And see a far off shining star

To sit and watch scenes like this
Gives one piece of mind
A feeling of contentment
God's gifts to all mankind

These are the simple things of life
Yet, something money cannot buy
To put a value on these things
I would not even try.

A J Bell

JOURNEY TO THE DARKER WORLD

Fire upon fire
A distant moon glow
Mountain on horizon
As white as winter snow.

        Wolves in forests waiting
        Yellow cold in eyes
        She saw the heated hillside
        As the southside dragon flies.

Iced lake that travelled north
Upon the grassy ways
To take the icy fishes
And carry them for days.

        Explosions in the darkness
        Of a bright and honest colour
        To drown out all the saddest news
        That made her life seem duller.

So watching from her lonely tree
She saw the darker world pass by
Taking all her concentration
She flew towards the sky.

Kiri Bashford

ONE WEE GIRL'S POEMS

One wee girl's poems were terribly gummy,
If you read them with jam they went to your tummy.
She wrote them in day,
She wrote them in night.
Then one time she was writing,
She got a terrible fright!
One of her poems danced on the page,
One of her poems went grey with age.
With her *scream* she screamed down the whole house,
And the whole country too,
All because of a poem or two!

Suzanne Al-Gayaar

ALL YOU GAVE ME

When I was only little
You gave me wings, so I could fly
And as you painted on each colour
Showing the way to reach so high
As the tiny wings unfolded
And grew stronger everyday
Revealing all you'd painted
To set me on my way
I felt so very special
Cocooned by all your love
Giving me the inner strength
To soar and rise above
Now everyday reveals more colours
Though my wings are slightly worn
But they show me, all you gave me
On the day that I was born
What you gave has more real value
Than a pocketful of gold
As gold slips through our fingers
You placed love in my heart to hold.

Kim Martin

MEMORIES

Memories of happy days
Beside the River Clyde
Picnics with the children
Then strolling side by side.

Watching ships sail up and down
An ever constant stream
Alas the days of many ships
Are now a long lost dream.

We built ships and we sailed in them
And crossed the oceans wide
Carry various cargoes
As from port to port we plied.

The River Clyde is quiet now
Ships few and far between
But we still have proud memories
Britannia, and the Queen's
The Portonian.

William McCann

CALAIS

Seven old biddies went across the sea
We didn't go by ferry
We went by Channel 'T'

We didn't go to Paris
We went to Calais Cite
Where we had omelette for dinner
And chips (They call Pomme Fritte)

We wandered round and round and round
Through galleries galore
Then bought our wine in Tesco
And our cheeses in Carreforr

And when we thought that Calais
Had seen enough of us
We slowly made our way home
To join our homeward bus

We settled down with sandwiches
Left over from before
The 'G & T' was wonderful
We would have liked one more

But we're sensible old biddies
So all we had to say
Was 'Au revoir to Calais
We had a lovely day'.

P Chamberlain

MIST OF DOOM

Inviting and creeping quietly,
Laying a circle over everything in its path,
Coming in to attack,
As it curls like a ball of fluff.

Smothering you with its musty aroma,
Gagging for breath - heart pumping,
Panic arising, eyes blurred,
Heart whines as the beats are missing,
The light has blown the body still,
Death, death echoes.

Elaine Barnes

SOLDIER

Leaning against foreign soil
A bank of mud, cold fear
Staring at a precious photograph
Of a faraway life
Wishing you could return
Distant fireworks crash through your head
Death dancing nearer
Taunting you in this maze of blood
Screamed out prayers of desperate men
Float to your ears
Your comrade in arms crying in silence
Crouched beside you
Wishing for divine help and protection
The way you have done a hundred times before
The waltzing fireworks draw near
And the boy beside you
Goes to another battleground
Watching this danse macabre before your eyes
You wonder what it's all really for
Dying in a land God has forgotten.

Jenna McDevitt (15)

RAINBOWS ROUND MY FEET

When umber shadows slide across the moon
And flood my wall with dancing silhouettes
Who will care for me?
Who will chase the boggarts of the nights
And stay the whirling charcoal flits.
And who will mend my kite
The one with orange tails
That swish and flail and spin and dive
On lumpy winds.

And who will mend my yacht?
Where mast and sail are a tangled disharmony
Of knotted twine and splintered shivers.
That deny my blistered thumbs.
And who will tie my lace so that
I may kick the stones with all my might
Through oily puddles,
Spraying rainbows round my feet.

When will I hear the skylark sing sharp and clear
High on Barley Moor.

Will the summer ever come again?

Hayes Turner

REMEMBERING

Your memory is the sweetest thing that I could ever hold
The love that lives within my heart is never ever told
I'm missing you my darling with each and every day
Pretending you are near to me in work as well as play

The gift of life for fifteen years were the best we ever had
Sometimes so full of laughter, sometimes so awfully sad
But when I see you darling through the windows of my mind
I see you as a treasured girl, a very special kind

I wonder why he took you, it's hard to understand
With rapists, thieves and murderers living throughout the land
He took you my dear daughter far, far, far too soon
If He had only let you live you would have reached the moon.

T Wood

ONE LITTLE BIRD

Look down the path, craggy and old,
They sky is so blue, the sun looks like gold,
The breeze is so gentle, it flickers the grass,
Birds flying gracefully, as over they pass,
Stop and listen, not a sound to be heard,
Only the chirping of one little bird.
Rabbits hop merrily, feeling so free,
A squirrel scampers across and runs up the tree,
Stop and listen, not a sound to be heard,
Only the chirping of one little bird.
The water it glistens as it wanders along,
One little bird still singing its song,
Rejoice in the beauty, worries will cease,
A feeling of harmony, a feeling of peace,
Stop and listen, not a sound to be heard,
Only the chirping of one little bird.

E M Gough

THERE - WITH YOU

I sit alone, my conscience deep,
my thoughts are lost and far away,
they lie with you when you're asleep,
to kiss you when you start your day.

And so you see, 'My heart's still there,'
although still gripping on so tight,
not letting go, to show I care,
though missing you throughout the night.

I close my eyes to hold you near,
a loving feeling, just we two,
and when my thoughts become so clear,
I'm not alone, 'I'm there - with you'.

Alan Holmes

YOU HAVE TO GO

There are times in many relationships when
No matter how deep the attachment or how close the emotional tie,
The alliance just has to end.

One of you has got to go.

Over my lifetime I've left a lot of relationships.
The first was my family;
Then, school, jobs and marriage.
From one to the other, believe me,

It's easy to leave.

You feel pangs of guilt at first but after a while,
Leaving becomes a pattern, a simple process, as you go with a smile.

However, this time, I can't go my dear.
This time, I must tell you to leave.
I know! I feel the ache you feel.
But I'm also aware of what we've both known for a long time.
For you've been with me longer than anyone.
Longer than my husband and as long as each and every child.

I have known you and come to love you longer than anyone else.
I have also accepted your protection from all the slings and arrows
That life's rejections and hurts have dealt me.
You have sheltered me from each and every blow.

The only thing you can't protect me from is you.

I've been able to carry you around with relative ease for many years.
Up until now, the comfort you provided me with made the weight
                                        of you unnoticeable.
But lately, you've grown to a size that even I, with my love and
                                        need for you,
Simply cannot bear any longer.

When I drag you up the stairs, I can hardly breath.
When I try to run, you hurt my knees.
Sometimes, when I lie down, the weight of you causes my heart
                                                    to pound.
I know you do not mean to cause this pain or the agony of
                                                    my decision;

Sister Fat, it's time for you to go.

Lee Makarov

SEASON'S TURN

Even the crows are
in on it, black

against a darkening
sky

as the wind turns to
September.

The season's turn
is

Crows' turning to black,
wind's lifting of leaves

a shadowing blow. The crow
flaps free. Light thickens.

J Copping

MY LOVE

(Written to my lover)

I only wish that you could read the circles of my mind,
Then you would know my thoughts of love were not totally confined
To hearts and flowers, but deep, true and meaningful words of love
That I declare to you.

I only wish that you could see my sincerity of mind,
No thoughts impaired, no false delusion,
But truth and honesty, no mass confusion,
Purity for you to find.

I only wish that you could see the image that you hold,
The pedestal so high and proud, the ground below belief untold,
You offer me your life with love
Our love, no lies between us told.

I only wish that you could see, just how hard I strive,
To make you glance and notice me, to smile and
Just acknowledge me,
To look beyond my face, my voice, to see my love is life.

Kim Higgins

I AM ME

To the changlings of fashion,
And the monarchs of the state,
Who think I should be thankful,
That I should fit a dress size eight.

That my hair should be this colour,
And the golden tan I fake,
Is not from expensive holidays,
Which I do not choose to take.

To everyone who knows me,
And everything I do,
Would things have been done different,
If the spotlight was on you.

That I should act improper,
And not adhere to rules,
That I surround myself with idiots,
Criminals and fools.

To those who profess to know
How we should live our lives,
And are horrified to find
A single woman strive

To keep her maiden name,
Or to gain a PhD,
That the boundaries of tradition,
Could be modified by me.

To one who has to live
Through the havoc I create,
From the comprehensive teacher,
To the sullen reprobate.

I dare them now to bask
In my reflected glory,
Not to analyse my life,
Or to publish my life story.

And if the present pass me by,
Or the future bears no fruit,
If those elusive seeds of knowledge
No longer will take root.

Gail McDonald

REMEMBER

This for all the young men who died in vain
All who endured death, despair and pain.
Those who couldn't continue the carnage
And lost their minds in the mud-filled trenches.
Duty turns our thoughts to but once a year
On the eleventh hour we shed a tear.
What youngster knows a red poppy's parade?
To them just another boring charade.
We could better honour their memory
To think on events of their century.
As I write this on a computer screen
I know nothing of the Hell they have seen.

Mark Cope

MOTHER NATURE

It is your seeding tree,
The moon watches as it wanes,
Prepare for daybreak,
Dawn is the sun's rebirth.

One seed of natural conception,
No hybrids.
Sometimes the sky blushes,
Then you shall have your shower.

Self dispersal throughout the world,
Yet the sequence carries on.
To break the daisy chain and become life,
This I wish upon you,
As a bright light falls through the sky.

It is time to bloom,
Take my hand and I will show you how to become.
Petals of wild colour,
Released into the field,
No further.

Deborah Berne

AQUA PARC

David Hockney poolshine
Net, - wideover see-through blue,
Tangling butterfly strokes.

A throw - in breath crawl, rising
To surfaces . . . near straw
mushrooms, parasol pine trees -

In a chlorine - vague shrine,
Palatial - tiled, sun-high,
PVC snakes downslope.

- hiss at smart or fast talk,
Conversations shallow,
- slow - worm to puddle-deep.

Lorna Liffen

THE DANCE

She steps into footprints deep in the sand,
moving her body to the pattern they weave,
listening to the voices singing their song,
capturing the shadows before they leave.

As the gypsy beat starts to liven its tempo,
figures sway wildly like branches in a breeze,
seductive motions make shapes in the moonlight,
it controls her being and begins to tease.

The midnight air is now getting much colder,
but the fire that burns is still very strong,
trepidation has reached its dizzy height,
it kidnaps her mind and the dance goes on.

Suzy Boon

PICTURES OF YOU

Pictures of you.
Three moments caught in amber,
Honey-tinted, seen through retrospective eyes.

Pictures of you.
Static, but unfurling in memory.
And prone to fade, as memories will.
But not just yet.

Pictures of you.
Laughing, mirth stopped mid-motion.
Sitting, eyebrows beetled with a pensive, quizzical stare.
Gazing out with a look that might be love . . .
But probably isn't.

Pictures of you.
Brief happiness then, recorded.
And seen now with a half-smile of half-remembered good times.
Of having had something wonderful . . .
And letting it slip right through your fingers.

Tsui-Ling Yu

KISS ME TO HEAVEN

When lovers lie awake at night
Not knowing what to do
The only thing important
Is just to be with you

How could our words paint pictures
Of how feelings really feel
When holding close so tenderly
Our love is all so real

You keep on asking questions
Like a detective on the case
And then you start to cackle
At the look upon my face

And so we started laughing
Tomorrow chuckles more
As we remember the odd phrase
That we whispered on the floor

I think about you daily
In a hundred different ways
And look so forward to our meeting
That I even count the days

Kiss me to Heaven Woman
I want to go there with you
Kiss me to Heaven Woman
You've taught me that Heaven is true.

Frank Samet

THE WATER SKIER

You whisk me careening past bright orange markers,
barely aware of a beach through the spray;
families fold away blankets and hampers,
and slaked on sunshine they slip from the day.

Back in the sands my thermos mourns,
lid screwed tight lest its dreams should all spill;
heart almost cold - the lengthening shadows
are claiming the evening scavengers' kill.

White foam in the flush of your aftermath - shivering
and choking on turmoil I cling to your tale;
though your hair billows black at the lip of a dwindling
sun, still I reach for one sip of that grail.

Chris Sherlock

TO WHOM IT MIGHT CONCERN

Who do I complain to, where do I get an answer
Who chose your life to crop and burn, who gave you your cancer

Who put decay inside you, who was friendly while they mock
Whose caress betrayed a promise and now the ticking of a clock

Whose love is dust and sickness that will take away your breath
Whose frameless name, whose unfelt shame has sentenced you to death

Why pick her for company, I'll fall on the sword
Why not take my defiled sin, my blood is bored

Why when she excels every mortal thing
Will you take her name, her favour and the joy that she can bring

Will you reconcile the pain of her family and friends
Will we weep no more and sleep, will sorrow never end

When her unborn children echo softly through the flame
When her heart is set free will she remember my name

When she's gone who now will speak my worth
Whatever her place of rest she's too good for that earth

Whatever her disease it makes my body ill
Whatever her religion for this they have no pill

So where is her God now! To reward the years of prayer
That prostitutes their trade for fame and this is the bill she has to pay
With bloody hands he'll kidnap her to a place I'll never view
Revenge is my conquering power and I am in the queue

Paul Stuart

CONVERSATION PIECE

Well look who's here, how are you now?
Have you recovered from your op?
I didn't expect to see you again.
Off I thought you'd pop.

You did look ill when I saw you last,
you looked a real old crock.
To think that you are still around.
You've given me quite a shock.

Old Mrs Brown's not well again.
The doctor's been today.
There's not much hope for her this time.
As least, that's what they say.

My sister's ill but she struggles on,
though you may well ask me how.
You remember how she used to be?
Well, you wouldn't know her now.

I haven't been too good myself.
I really need a rest.
It's a good job I'm a cheerful sort.
I could easily get depressed.

But it's nice to see you once again,
though you're still not looking right.
You'll have to take care of yourself
if your future's to be bright.

I've quite enjoyed our little chat.
Would you like another cup?
I hope you'll come again next week.
It will help to cheer you up.

Brian Hunt

MEMORY BOX

In a dark corner of my house stands an enormous cupboard with huge varnished doors and a matt finish. Every so often I visit it and touch the old brass handles. They are not cold to the touch, but warm and comforting. They curl silent hands around me and tug gently at my shirt as I go to open the heavy doors. With a gentle sigh of satisfaction the worn old mahogany door swings open, and inside a smaller more delicate box lies glowing.

It has a painstakingly made velvet lining, and softened edges, seeming to make little but a slight glitch in the space around it. Carefully I lift the prized gift and flip the bronze clips up. Nervously pulling on the lid of my memory box until it slides open.

Tall trees nurture a young mind,
As soldiers of virtue play on grassy lawns.
Stories of adventure are told by a
Wise old armchair,
Gently rocking me to sleep.
Anger and frustration are tamed,
By a fascination with all things living.
A musty smell of beaten clothing
And a well-tanned hand,
Helping along the way.

A cry of muffled tears pushed into broadened shoulders,
Till next time,
When bonds are rigged and fastened,
Before sailing away in a small toy boat.

I see everything for a split second, and then it is gone, and there is nothing I can do to get it back.

Joe Langfeld Flory

I WANT TO BREAK FREE

What is it they want from me?
They want me to understand where they're coming from
Want me to solve everything
Can't they see I just want to be free

Free from expectations
Free from others' problems
Free from a fake ID
Free to be me

To live my life for myself
Be who I want to be
To go out into the big, wide world
And find my own wealth

Not to live in others' shadows
Or act out someone else's life
Just be myself, is what I want to be
I wish they would just see

I'm not just here for others
I've got to be here for myself
To solve my own problems
And not using others as a cover

I don't need comparisons
To feel a greater or lesser person
Just accept me for my ability
Just accept me for being me

Maybe I'll fail
Maybe I won't
But does it really matter
Just give that boat a chance to sail

Let me be free
Let me do it my way
I don't know if I can do it
But at least let me try

I'm not who you want me to be
I'm not who I want me to be
But this is who I am
So give me a chance

I'll prove that you can trust me
I'll try my best to prove I can succeed
But I live my life for me
And finally break free.

Naomi Sambrook

INSIGNIFICANT OTHER

Talk all you want, waste your breath
Too many lies to get off your chest
Scream and shout, can't be heard
You had your lessons but didn't learn
Know your name, you're not friends
The game is yours but the rules are bent
Just enough rope, too close to the ground
The hope you've lost will not be found
Large as life, can't be seen
Making progress - can't succeed
You're left behind, all your fault
Pick a wound - pour the salt
Broken hearts, shattered dreams
Your perfect world has split its seams
Cry all night, crocodile tears
Not scared enough to face your fears
Beaten down, looking up
Force it open, slam it shut
Have no faith, on your knees
Despise your own hypocrisy
It all broke down, you came apart
That jilted lover took your heart
Spent your soul, made to suffer
Bet you thought that you were tougher
Not forgiven, just forgotten
Unrequited, misbegotten.

Michael Fraser

MY NATASCHA

My Natascha the young
fine looking and very vibrant young lady
who dwells in my heart and dreams
and that my love for Natascha will
never fade away into darkness.

My dreams of Natascha are
always driven with such wild goings
on that my love for Natascha belongs
to fairy tales, you see I'm her prince on
horseback and she's my sweet fair maiden
dressed in white satin and lace.

My Natascha is an image
of beauty with her short Copper
Brown hair, Golden tanned skin which
by touch is like the finest silk and her
eyes of blue, also her slim body, also her face of
an angel which could command the gates of Heaven
to open and that Natascha will always be in my dreams.

Richard Bloor

A KY Christmas

To the disco beat of dance floor grooves,
Ray-mond, 'The Stud', tries out his moves.
With a full spin turn, carefully perfected,
He claps, points . . . and has to be respected!
In leopardskin thong, then tight black trousers,
He knows he's wearing babe arousers!
Then slipping on his batwing shirt,
He can't wait to score, with all the skirt.
A splash of aftershave, then aerosol scent,
He knows that he is heaven sent.
With Rolex watch and gold medallion,
He's a deadly disco, roving stallion!
Cool, sophisticated, totally in charge,
Ray-mond 'The Stud' is now at large.
Entering the arena, in confident fashion,
He's looking for love and rampant passion.
He takes his time and the night moves on,
But 'The Stud' is waiting, for, 'The One'.
Then just as things start to slow,
There she is . . . It's time to go.
Sidling over, feeling like James Bond,
He approaches a beautiful strawberry blonde.
'Would you like to dance?' he asks, with confident air.
'No . . . my husband's over there!'
Graciously he backs away,
Unlucky in love this Christmas Day.
Soon, the revellers start to leave
But there is no one on his sleeve.
At home he rues his cruel luck
Where will he get a Christmas . . . !
In a ductless drawer, a favourite mate,
Will have to do for his Christmas date.

John Wilcock

MODIFIED

On the night of New Year's Eve
An old battle tank rumbles
Silently through city streets
To appear unseen at the Cenotaph

The guns lower like sulky dogs,
The hatch opens, and speaking
As he always does to those
Who will not listen -
He says -
'You have modified my dreams,
Dammed up the streams with silk and money
You have taken my greatcoat
And shoved it in the moat round your
    museums
You have spoiled all my sons
Made them thumbs without a finger -
And on this night of millennial death
Your putrid reeking breath
Is not worthy of the gases
And the flowers of the Somme.'

Peter Asher

MOTHER'S BOX

My mother weeps over a wooden box
Not the polished one in which Hannah lies
But the one that's upstairs with two padlocks
Which sometimes she opens with burning eyes
Flooding her head with that terrible night
Whilst clutching to her a dress of smoked white.

Wishing and praying that things were not so
And something could crush the hurt and the pain
She hears the shrill screams with her breath now low
And still feels the heat and scorching of flames
Time's a great healer or so someone says
Her hands on the dress her mind in a daze.

If only she'd thought, if only she'd said
She's sure it would not have happened at all
But what's past is gone, her daughter stays dead
Hannah has answered her heavenly call
Don't keep the box Mum, let memories fade
Demons of torment eternally laid.

Maybe she needs to recall now and then
Her little girl's life snatched by the fire
But I can't help hoping, wondering when
That box will go to its own funeral pyre
Though not quite yet as Mother wipes her tears
And upstairs it goes for a few more years

Andrew Roe

SIGH OF RELIEF

For hours, for days, the rain kept coming down
The river twisting and turning toward the small town.
Expanding its size with each hour that passed by
As ever more rain fell down from the sky.
Then jumping its banks in a blind fit of rage
It was like a wild animal let loose from its cage.
Gushing and spewing where it chose to go
Knowing nothing could stop its wild surging flow.
Engulfing and sweeping all from its path
With each surge of water, I heard the beast laugh.
Over the fields, through gardens it ran
Proving to all it was stronger than man.
Streaming through doorways this monster flowed on
Ensuring that each man's possessions were gone.
Pouring and flooding and swirling around
This unstoppable force soon conquered the town.
Then it stopped, just as suddenly as it began
Deciding to return this place back to man.
Retreating along its once raging path
With more of a giggle than a deep roaring laugh.
Returning to the place from whence it came
Knowing the town could never be the same.
Returning to slumber, till woken again
To rise and destroy all things treasured by men.

In the millennium year Mother Nature awoke
Did you hear her whisper when she finally spoke?

John Cobban

THE HOLLY BUSH CAFÉ

There's a café in the town, where we love to sit down,
We take tea with scones and fresh cream,
A welcoming smile from the waitress with style
And the cook with long hair looks like Jesus.

The Holly Bush Café is the place to be seen,
To dine there is simply a dream,
Glossy wood panels with posters of puzzles attempt to cover the past,
The style of the place is not in the race of life in the city somewhere.

Attached to the house, the café juts out, a picture so English and quaint,
Displayed on a stand the menu so grand, of spiced soup and
beef en croute,
Sweet apple pie takes to the eye of every Burway hiker,
Take your time over dinner in summer or winter, feast full to the
music of Bach.

What more can be said of a place to be fed,
That has charm and a small kind of grandeur,
Stretton folk sit down drinking tea, have a chat,
Take your time, there's no race, as we gaze through
The window, at Holly Bush Café.

Harry Bates

WITHOUT LOVE

The warmth in a touch,
The softness of a stroke,
His hands caressing my body.
We share a heartbeat,
But I'm really alone, sinking in my seat.

Loneliness causes me so much pain.
I'm alone, forever alone.
I walk through the streets in the pouring rain.
I'm alone, forever alone.

A male to cure this pain is what I desire,
But every man I've met is a compulsive cheat and liar.
To feel like this is to feel empty of life.
I don't want not be a mother, mistress or wife,
Just in a relationship of two,
Him and me that would do.

To feel wanted, to feel loved,
That's the most powerful feeling in the world.
But I've never had it.

I can't feel the warmth of a touch
Or the softness of a stroke,
There's no one to share my heartbeat.

I'm alone, forever alone.

Carman

A Summer's Day

A beautiful day no clouds to be seen
The heat from the sun pours down.
I'm lying here at the water's edge
Away from the bustle of town.

I see people with prams, pensioners too
All pass by to take in the view.
Children playing without a care
Watchful mothers always there.

Ducks noisily pass by
Their young in a line, follow afloat,
The river is theirs on this warm day
They do not mind a passing boat

Squirrels chatter in the trees
See the people as they pass,
Ever watching just in case
A snack is dropped in the grass.

The clouds appear as the day grows old
The people are here no more,
I too must be on my way
Perhaps to another shore.

Carol Alton

DEATH

Wheels in the great clock of Time
Whirl, as years like seconds, chime
Round and round through shrinking hoops,
Mankind toddles, runs, then stoops

Death, your pendulum's a knife
Each fresh tick, cuts off a life.

Sheena Blackhall

THREE TOWNS IN THE NORTH-WEST

I'll tell you now, so listen and bear witness,
No one should have to live in Widnes -
The smell from the place is nobody's business.
The chemicals there scare me shit . . . witless.
I'm telling you - no one should have to live in Widnes.

I'll tell you something else, don't look forlorn,
I'm not really that fussed on Runcorn
Either. Despite its castle - well, most of that's gorn.
A heritage site now - it's been reborn
Not a lot else to be said, about Runcorn.

Here's a tip, and it's not the price of melons,
No one should be forced to study in St Helens.
It's main claim to fame is that Colin Welland's
So, as Shakespeare once said, 'All's well that . . . well ends,'
Though I don't think he came from St Helens.

David Howard

FOR JIMMY YOUNG

(BBC broadcaster and one time singer)

Back in the 1950's
When Jim was all the rage
I used to take my panties off
And throw them on the stage
But thro' the years
I've grown and grown
Old Jim is still a 'wow'
My bloomers they would knock him flat
If I should throw them now.

Wendy Joiner

RUBY WEDDING

*(To my wonderful mum and dad on this special day
with lots of love.)*

Forty years as husband and wife
Sharing four decades of each other's lives
Building a home and family
To achieve the best for you and me.

Like the pages of a story each chapter appears
Some make you laugh others bring tears
But through it all one thing is clear
You still love each other in this fortieth year.

As you walked down the aisle rock and roll
topped the charts
And sprinkled some magic into both of your hearts
So here's to memories old and memories new
Happy anniversary to both of you.

Lynsey McGowan

CHRISTMAS

All is still
A star shines bright
There is a kind of hush over the world tonight
A kind of expectancy not known before
Look yonder - a donkey outside a stable door
Tethered to a stake the poor old thing
Something is happening there within
What's that I hear - a baby's first cry
So different from any other
When it's first separated
From its mother
Suddenly the sky is alight
Like a brilliant day at the dead of night
What is there in that stable
That can make the world so changed
Just a little baby
Jesus is his name
He is awake in a manger on a bed of straw
Who is that child lying in that stall?

P Ellwood

MUNGUS

When we saw you Peachy dear
With all the other kittens,
You looked so ill and scrawny
But you had lovely white mittens.

We chose your sibling to take home
A beautiful little kitten
But all our eyes returned to you,
At once we all were smitten.

So that day we arrived back home
With two naughty little kittens,
The first thing that we did was to
Change the name you were given.

Mr Perkins your brother did not live long,
A car accident saw to that.
O how you suffered on your own
You just sat and sat and sat!

Over the eighteen years you lived with us,
Jake and Monty came as well,
But as with your brother, Mr Perkins,
They were taken from us too.

Now we just had you Mungus,
Our ginger and white fur ball,
Your hearing and eyesight failing
But you were still loved by all.

Your nature was so gentle,
The children you never scratched,
They'd pick you up and love you
As you looked and loved them back.

Christine Blayney

GRASSHOPPER

There wouldn't be a blade of grass for kilometres
on show at the conference in the Dark Vaulted Theatre
like a trick of nature

video cameras are researching our schooled faces
our hands palm down on our papers on the melting table
our shuttered eyes staring down the limelight for later

he lands with a spring-loaded click on my paper
out of the colour of the Australian veldt
complete

the camera is reading our encounter
so we speak.

Jennifer Compton

ON VAN GOGH'S 'THE POTATO EATERS'

'Van Gogh mad?' they said.
Yet what a revelation of realism
Is to be seen in 'The Potato Eaters'.
These humble peasants
In no way romanticised,
Devour their mean rewards
For a grim life
Of drudgery and sweat,
That is indelibly imprinted
In their gnarled hands.
Their impassive faces identify them
With the earth; for of the earth they were.
For them there was no hope;
Mere existence was their lot.

They were a tribute to one
Whose deep feelings for humanity
Flowed into paint;
The medium he mastered.

Ina J Harrington

HIS SPIRITUAL ANGEL

She appeared from nowhere
Wearing wings by the pair
Full of spiritual presence and fun
With an insight second to none
Ready to help a lost sole
So he could help others in a hole
In all kinds of ways
To be a good listener it pays
But angels can become unwell
Whom do they go and tell
His spiritual angel has spoken
Her silence she has broken
Now therapy is the occupation of their choice
Listen to his and her voice
Lifelong happiness seemed a never
Love and kisses forever and ever.

Steve Lattimore

THE ENLIGHTENMENT

All night I lay awake
Restless, trying to sleep
But sleep eluded me
A vigil, I must keep

As I lay there waiting
Thoughts flew into my head
Elusive and fleeting
Things I had read and said

Then something strange happened
I can hardly explain
But I knew something had
Never, the same again

I was filled with power
More an enlightenment
I could do anything
Wherever my thoughts went

I could solve my problems
I could solve world problems
I was filled with wisdom
I had the answers to them

Wide awake and alive
Tingling with new power
With all senses sharpened
I was aglow for hours

I focused my thoughts on
A particular thing
In seconds it was solved
I could solve anything.

When the pale light of dawn
Shone over my body
Ready to face the day
Alas! I was a nobody.

Terry Daley

WHAT ELSE

Jewels and finest horse
Golden trays and silver cups
Swinging from the place roof
To a song my lover sings
She might be as poor as me
But I'm the king of kings

What else is there on Earth
That I would rather possess
All I need is her
I care not for the rest.

Pebbles and white horses
Perfect sand and rising stars
All the world's a castle
Bow down to her song
She's all I ever need
All day and all night long.

Rodger Moir

NOW, THEN AND FOREVER

You say you can't stop time
when you watch that miniature sailing ship
whirl gently from your ceiling
when you look into the eyes of
the plush lion cub
standing atop the set of drawers
when you listen to that catchy tune
that strikes a nostalgic chord inside your bones
when you play with the bauble
that's like a rose window
which you call an oil puzzle
and see how the colors form and flow
casting sensuous shadows
do you not in a fashion
bend the concept of time?
So, for Heaven's sake stop complaining about
the hours, the months, and the years that go by
re-lent-less-ly
Oh, you are getting old, aren't you?
And your skin wrinkles, your back aches
and your teeth gnash
have you forgotten the growth pains of the adolescent
your first period, all that blood gone wasted?
The cycle goes on
you maintain
yes it does, and you become
the seed from which
a new generation will grow
the fertiliser of youth
Is that not time resuscitated?

Albert Russo

CAGED

The lion lay resigned
In his small square cage
A look of hopeless emptiness
In eyes, once that blazed

His coat was scanty and mottled
His skin showing through in places
As I looked, his eyelids slowly closed
They said, 'I am in this terrible place.'

Once free and roaming wild
The good gold earth was mine
I crept and stalked and lived a life
Of happy wandering.

Now here I am demented,
By daily gazing on me,
No place to hide or shelter
Away from the madding throng.

I want to be free and running
In Africa's veld and sun
To roam and see the splendour
Of my heritage, now long since gone.

Replaced by an iron cage
For numerous eyes to see
Me deprived of splendour
Who did capture me?

Jean Bald

ORGANISATIONAL SKILLS OF A LADY

Yes, but I haven't got any!
I wouldn't like to be like my bloody friend
Who's over the top about everything she has
As though everything has a place.

I don't stay awake at night
Like she does the Martha misery of her life
Worrying about trivial things,
Like some kind of masquerade
Of her life's hang-ups.
And this woman is a therapist!

Does she tidy her patients in the same way?
Definitely a case of verbal diarrhoea.

I lead a life of disorganisation.
I now have stress for breakfast, lunch and tea.
Fortunately that's me.

Sean Conway

BACK IN DOUBT (NO COMPROMISE)

Nervous system broken down,
Spinal cord cut and ripped out,
Eyes torn from blind dismay,
Lips sealed to swallow decay.

Skin and bone burnt to corrode,
Flesh and blood drained as death's ode,
Fingers severed for stealing truth,
Heart slashed for finding proof.

Senses down and feeling drowned,
Brain slowly brought back into doubt.
Life lingering over the halo of night,
Alone and unloved; there is no comprise.

Helen Marshall

THANK YOU XX

When I think of passion
I think of you
When I think of togetherness
I feel hopelessly blue
When I think of crying
My eyes draw the shade
When I think of dying
You're at my aid
When I think of possession
I gave you my heart
When I think of your influence
It pulls me apart
When I think of our love
Those were my greatest years
When I think of the future
My love turns to tears
When I think of your laughter
It brings a smile to my face
When I think of what we had
Nothing can take its place
When I think of your beauty
Delightful was its form
When I think of the past
It does excite and warm

Warren Brown

SONNET TO A CHILD WITH CHARACTER

I like your figure: lithe, and full of grace,
The sprightliness with which you bounce and skip;
I like the clarity in your bright face,
That tilted head, the minute teeth, firm lip.

When still a baby, you could outstare me
With solemn gaze . . . and I would lose my nerve
To turn my eyes, vanquished, while you stayed free -
Yet I had hoped your sweet smile to deserve.

At four years old, you're independent, strong.
Though learning all the time, it's you who lead.
You chatter, play, throw tantrums, stump along . . .
When stubborn, you're impossible to feed.

Small child: I worship you. Behold your slave!
Your gracious favour is all that I crave.

Katharine Holmström

ON PRODUCTIVITY AND PROGRESS

Out of ideas hundred
Which in our minds delve
We finally follow up
Only ten, maybe twelve.

And of those chosen few
On which we proceed
Only one, or just two
Ultimately succeed.

But even when these
Do materialise
They don't perfectly please -
We do soon realise.

Hence take care, my friends
In choosing your trends
So that when each one ends
You'll have huge dividends.

Kopan Mahadeva

A LETTER TO THE HEART

Didn't I tell you to stop breathing last night?
It's the morning, you're still alive,
Do I have to put a knife through you to realise?
Don't you know I don't love my life?
Wake up with a heavy heart,
Going to sleep feeling apart,
Nothing to look forward to,
Apart from hurt, pain and more,
I feel so defeated,
Tears spring from my eyes,
But never seem to wash away the pain of heart,
Nobody really understands why I suffer like this?
I wake up feeling like a rock,
Being crumbled in one's hand,
Dying, dying, away from the sunlight.

Shakti-Devi

Once Upon A Dream

The beautiful rose has thorns which have been
scrubbed across my body,
some embedding themselves deep within my back.
The enchanting castle has locked me inside,
its most deepest, darkest dungeon with rats and roaches
that run across me in their millions.
The magnificent winged unicorn who carries me up
across the many skies has fiery breath and a nature
as evil as the scars on my face.
I cannot run
I cannot escape.

Jenita Bhudia

FREEDOM

Not expected
nor
necessarily aware
of the craving for.

But accepted
finally
without grace
or want

With a slow,
calling grin
from the centre
of my soul.

Odelia Schaare

MY CHILDHOOD GARDEN

Memories of a garden,
    Of summers long since gone,
When every day was make-believe,
    The sun forever shone.

Childhood days are fleeting,
    Like shadows on a lawn,
All happiness and laughter
    Bequeathed to life unborn.

Now roses cease to ramble,
    No children's voices call,
And ghosts frequent the silent trees,
    Alas, the leaves must fall.

J M Armstead

FLUTE

My sounds pierce the air like a bird of the dawn.
I play when she requests me to be played,
A pipe of contrasts, smoking puffs of tune.

Brown shelves, green books shine from my body
As I lie on the piano, a delicate tube
Sleeping, to be awakened by her lips.

White and grey shapes float in a blue sky;
The birds sing sweeter songs than mine.
A sorrowful, melancholy, graceful melody

Flows from deep within. Sharp forced notes
When angry. Chocolates, radio, me,
Alone in a world full of creatures is she.

Open-minded, intelligent, I eagerly await that time
When I once again will sing a playful tune;
Minor keys have had their day.

Exhausted from countless empty hours,
She sighs to a world without ears and stares
Through the clear sheet at that pale ball

In a distant black blanket.
It can hear my music no more
Than the others on this earth except her.

The candles are flickering dots in the keys
Of my slender frame, showing pale cheeks
And a starved soul in a young body. We are delicate

But have the strength to go on.
Floating, inspiring, she breathes life into me
And I breathe life into her.

Jasminder Ghuman

WHEN I HAVE TIME

When I have time, so many things I'll do
To make life happier and much more fair.

For those whose lives are crowded, now with care
I'll help to lift them from their low despair
When I have time.

When I have time,
A friend will come and see them there,
And come to care.

I wish upon a star,
And when I come to wish upon that star
I often wonder how other people are
When I have time.

Chris Sterry

CHULA - TALE OF A SIAMESE CAT

I remember Chula
Our Siamese
Purring
And feeling warm fur on bedclothes
Attacking Father
But all in fun
With deadly claws
That brought home
Starlings
Mice
And other trophies
Tears
And weeping
From the busy road
Blue eyes
And snarling mouth
In deaths
Suspended animation
Grandfather muttering
'Poor old puss.'
'Poor old blacktail.'
Grave dug in garden soil
Wooden box coffin
And pebble
Marker.

Paul Wilkins

DELICATE ENCOUNTER

The summer was months away,
Yet she had captured
Its essence in sky blue eyes,
As she served fresh food.

Hair of apricot and gold,
Ample proportions,
Behind the counter of the
Delicatessen there.

Hands in plastic gloves were poised,
Grasping plastic tongs,
To pick up the ham to weigh,
Plump dimpled fingers.

There was a long queue waiting,
He daren't hang about,
Even though he wanted to
Invite her out sometime!

As he walked away it seemed
Suddenly darker,
His brightness had stayed with her,
Bonnie buxom lass.

Kathleen M Scatchard

WITHOUT THINKING

Without thinking, you can
make an awful trouble
for yourself.
Whereabouts, a moment's
thought, or a kind word
can avoid many a problem.

Should anyone walk into
your life,
and open their mouth
without thinking,
causing you to cry,
should you shed
a tear,
then it's time to say
goodbye!

Pauline Uprichard

ROBIN SWALLOWTAIL

In golden field of country bake
A waft of apple pie
A detour from the farm did make,
To greet a friend nearby.
Who, lonely as a windmill is,
Married to a pole,
A red glove and a blue glove and
Shoes which have no sole.
Fine countenance of cotton,
Rough shirt of bottle green,
All to oft' forgotten,
Often never seen . . .
And open as a can of beans
His hat, packed out with straw,
Old swallow-tailed his coat it seems,
Reaches to the floor.
With arms spread out like Jesus, thrice
Trousers tied with string . . .
Stands preaching to the carrion crow,
Round Robin in a ring.

Roger Mosedale

AND ENTERS

A simple day,
Innocent sail.

Wednesday, mid-week cup.
Alone, but lonely not.
Feeding on warm thoughts; darling, to a heart.

Just the thought,
And a smile, breaks flowing.

Sipping of pineapple juice,
Felt of contentment's massage.

Of contentment's massage.
Jealousies sinful!
And enters,
Giggly love birds.

Lazily raising the head,
Shocked! To cold silent wail.

Lord, let this, be a passing nightmare.
How could,
Why?
But . . .

Would have consoled,
But no;
As they passed, she looked into his eyes, smiling.
So much cruel beauty,
And dreams, come crashing.

But . . .
Gave her all.

When -Why - How?

The soul sobs;
Mercilessness having robbed, of full life.

Rowland Warambwa

NOMADS

Note: 'Bean Sidhe' Is A Gaelic Word pronounced 'Ban Shee'

What is it about the unworn track,
That frightens people so?
Is it the confusion? The darkness? The distortion?
The possibility of losing the way and becoming eternally lost
                    in the sea of travelling souls?
Yet are not these souls the ones who have gained?
Are they not the ones who have travelled their own path,
Created anew a sculpture,
Instead of merely chipping tiny flecks off the original art?
Are they not, eternal nomads as they may be,
Those who asked for adventure and had their wish granted
                    by some obliging star?
For these are those who have stood on the hill in a storm,
Felt the heavy torrents sting and curse the cheek,
Blinding, burning.
Heard the gales screaming like the Bean Sidhe in the ears,
Tugging at the hair, wrenching, tangling,
Have they not felt the chaos?
And yet,
Have they not found complete joy in that chaos,
A pure joy which cannot be found in anything but such adversity?
What good can one be if all he does is follow the rest?
Surely an individual energy, with a different slant, colour,
                    perception of the Divine is more beneficial?
And do we not agree that this true?
We do.
So I ask you,
Why do we persist in condemning these eternal nomads?
Why do we discriminate and force them away?
Pushing them beyond our reach, away from the light which
                    we see as salvation,

But in reality is merely damnation?
Their souls may be that of a nomad,
But in the end,
So is yours . . .

Kim Huggens

SCARECROW

In the field stark and bare,
Stands the man with his steely glare,
He never moves from his place,
The weather has made its mark on his face,
With ragged clothes and straw for hair,
His job is to be there to scare,
The seeds and crops he tries to protect,
The farmer comes to the field to inspect,
What he sees fills him with pride,
With a smile he turns to the arms stretched wide,
The birds he has helped to keep away,
His job is done for another day,
The crops can be gathered and put in store,
The scarecrow rests until he is needed once more.

Sandy

ARE WE ALONE?

I am a twig on that weird tree
and you are too. Are we ripe fruits?
Our roots are entwined. We are nourished
in the same soil. Are we all fallen,
metamorphosed angels? Milton almost
knows and Lamartine too. I collect
a souvenir from my past life,
you collect yours. Did Mephistopheles
nestle in that Golden Apple which
has consumed us as we are told?
Since then huge tears have welled up
in Gaea's eyes. The Tree of Knowledge
is still dripping mysteries, speaking loudly
of the First Sin, and relating tales of apples
picked, filled with smoke and fire.
From the bottom of Hades darkness
has risen up in our minds, yet light is still
flooding us. Eve is here, yet she is in eternity.
Look up at the sky. Billions of stars!
Are we alone in a shoreless universe,
or are there elsewhere other Eves
and Trees of Knowledge? Is all
the universe one cosmic tree of energy,
which is rooted in the Eternal Energy,
the Divine Force? Are all galaxies, suns
and planets but branches and foliage
with twigs some bearing fruits and some
bearing none? Are we sour or sweet fruits?
The Tree of Life renews itself as long as
Light exists. Vague shadows of a remote past
visit my imagination occasionally.
We all belong to one tree, one divine origin.
A new creation, another test, let's do our best.

Najwa Salam Brax

LONG DRIVE TO LOVE

Waiting for a flat
To pick me up
Outside the hospital gates
And take me to my darling's manger
I have yet to board one
And roar into infinity
To find them finally
After the long drive
Howling in the twilight
Of my wooded estate.

To enter the gates
The servants are waiting and ready
Already at my father's command
I greet him in his chamber with open arms
In the corner of the large room
Is a cedarwood floor of demonic mosaic
He will be a valuable asset.

It is time for supper
My grandmother must eat with us
And sits by my mother
Spring water is poured
Asparagus soup and bread brought
My darling rings for burning logs
Tomorrow I shall see my property by helicopter
There is smoke beneath the chestnuts
At the bottom of the lawn
We are together
Happy at last.

Victor Seymour

SAY YES TO LOVE

Love is an incredible thing
You don't need credit cards
You don't need fashion
Life is lively and full of fun
Using all the senses
Like children in a marathon.

Love is an incredible thing
Like our North East stars
Jimmy Nail, Sting, Robson Green,
Tim Healy, Denise Welsh, Kevin Whateley,
They all have been blessed
Love comes in all shapes and sizes
So let yourself be free
And have more faith in God.

Kenneth Mood

LOUD VOICES INN

I have thought, many a time,
In the hostelry, in which I recline,
Tis amusing to hear, the chatter,
Tis worse than the glasses,
They too, do clatter,
For me, that, does not matter.

When you see two in converse,
That cannot hear,
Whilst talking,
And sipping beer,
They laugh and shout,
At each other,
To try and get,
Their message over.

Still not hearing, what was said,
They scream at each other, their ears are dead,
'Earplugs' are wanted, when?
When 'they' are around
Sensitive ears
Cannot handle the sound.
To plug 'them' out, will make you great,
Free from deafness, and not irate.

A pair of earphones, not switched on,
'I promise,' will serve you well, with all aplomb,
You hear the converse in, tones well said,
And answer their questions,
Your drums are not dead.

George Theodore Harrison

HELP!

I'd like to help my fellow man
In any way, as best I can,
Not just with cash though that's a boon -
But with problems, causing gloom.

Two heads, they say, are better than one,
And that makes sense, battle's half won!
It doesn't need to cost money, to give
A helping hand, to someone with
A troubled life, maybe, an illness,
Or some small worry, that you witness.

Friends, family, yes, even foes,
We all of us have certain woes
That shared, become less of a burden,
That done! Maybe they will not worsen.

Winifred M Swann

INSIDE STORY!

So very little from here I see,
Oh what a situation - in which to be,
Shut away from soul and friend,
The days and nights in here I spend,
For a wrong I did - when in dire need,
Now in this cell, my heart does bleed,
None to hear - my cries of woe,
Shut away I hate it so,
I dream of fields, the skies above,
I dream of course of your true love,
I pray to He who dwells above,
Now I must go - as warder's shove,
From this soul, there's much to say,
But it is censored - in Holloway!

John L Wright

MARILYN

She wasn't just a pretty face
But a clever actress
Of style and grace
It takes more to be superstar
Than just a giggle and a wiggle.

Adrianne Jones